# How To Deal With
# Jealousy

**Taylor Timms**

**How To Deal With Jealousy**
by Taylor Timms

ISBN 978-1-926917-24-5

Printed in the United States of America

Copyright © 2010 Psylon Press

# Free Online Seduction Course

As a thank you for buying this book, I would like to give you access to my online women seduction course.

To claim your free spot, please go to
**www.foreverlaid.com**
and enter your valid email address now.

## Also by Taylor Timms

### Beautiful Breasts Pictures
ISBN 978-1-926917-01-6

### Top Bikini Pictures
ISBN 978-0-9866426-3-0

### Forever Laid Formula
Best Ways To Get Women To Sleep With You
ISBN 978-0-9866004-2-5

### Best Gift Ideas For Women
Perfect Gifts Ideas For Any Special Occasion
ISBN 978-0-9866004-4-9

# Table Of Contents

**Introduction**    7

**Chapter 1**    11
*What is Jealousy?*    12
*Loss Related Jealousy*    15
*Losing a Friend*    15
*Loss of Romantic Relationships*    16
*Loss of a Loved One who Has Died*    17
*Cheating and Betrayal*    18

**Chapter 2**    21
*Why People Feel Jealousy*    22
*Lack of Satisfaction*    23
*Understanding Rage*    25
*Understanding Trust*    27
*Understanding Self Esteem*    28

**Chapter 3**    29
*Entitlement and Reality*    30
*Understanding Reality*    31

**Chapter 4**    35
*The Consequences of Jealousy*    36

## Chapter 5                                    39

*Techniques for Overcoming Jealousy*            40
*Facing Reality*                                40
*Positive Thinking*                             41
*Understanding Comparison*                       43
*Acceptance*                                    45
*Elimination*                                   46
*When your Partner Has done*
*Nothing to Warrant Jealousy*                   49
*When your Partner Has Betrayed You*            58


## Conclusion                                   65


## Appendix 1                                   67


## Appendix 2                                   71


## Appendix 3                                   75


## Appendix 4                                   79


## Appendix 5                                   83


## Appendix 6                                   87

# Introduction

Jealousy is certainly nothing new to human nature but it has the potential to destroy relationships and make you miserable. Learning to understand what jealousy is, why you feel it and how to overcome it is essential. Whether you feel jealousy toward a co-worker or you experience romantic jealousy, it can be a dangerous emotion. While it may seem as though there is no way out, there are some techniques that you can use to avoid drowning within the depths of jealousy.

Jealousy can easily turn you into a person that you probably do not wish to be. Friends and family may begin to avoid you and there is little doubt that jealousy can cause your love life to suffer. While you may feel awful, you may also feel helpless to end the jealousy you experience.

Jealousy can be a tremendous burden and weight to carry around. It can easily overcome your life. Once you learn how to get rid of jealousy and get your emotions in check, you will be able to take back control of your life. Jealousy is something that everyone has experienced from time to time, even though you may not have ever admitted it to anyone else. It can be embarrassing, but now is the time to get the help you need and learn how to overcome jealousy once and for all.

In this guide, you will learn to understand how to effectively identify jealousy so that you can recognize it when it rears its ugly head. You will also learn about the different types of jealousy and how they can impact the various relationships in your life, including romantic and professional relationships. Additionally, you will learn techniques that you can use to overcome jealousy once and for all.

If you allow it, jealousy can easily take over and ruin your life. It does not have to be this way.

Are you ready to put jealousy behind you?

Let's get started!

# Chapter 1

# What is Jealousy?

Before we can begin to understand why we experience jealousy, it is important to first understand what it is that can make you jealous. If there was only one thing that ever made someone jealous in life, it would be relatively easy to determine the basis of jealousy, but that is not the case. It is critical to determine what it is that makes you jealous so that you can understand why you feel jealous.

When you experience jealousy, you most likely feel awful. Your entire life can feel as though it is falling down around you. Without a clear understanding of what is going on, it can be easy for every aspect of your life to be affected by the jealousy you feel. Jealousy can truly be a frightening experience. After you have learned what it is that makes you feel jealous, you will then be better equipped to understand why. That will give you the ability to relate it to other situations, so that you will be better prepared in the future to recognize potential problems before they become full fledged jealousy.

One of the most common reasons why people experience jealousy is related to material possessions. This can oftentimes be the root of jealousy in many instances. Feeling satisfied can often relate to material possessions and jealousy. Money can also relate to this type of jealousy. It is commonly human nature to assume that the more money an individual has, the more powerful they also are. Of course, this may not always be the case, but when you are an outsider looking into a situation, it can be easy to think that the person who has a lot of money also has a happy life. Whenever you see that someone has a new car, luxury home, designer clothing and other material items , it is fairly common to experience jealousy when you see that someone else has everything that you want but do not have the means to acquire.

This can create a feeling of inadequacy that may make you feel as though you do not measure of in any areas of your life. It is only natural for someone to want all of the good things in life and to feel bad when you see that someone else has them. These are the same feelings that you may have experienced as a child when a friend received a toy you wanted but did not have.

This materials possession form of jealousy is common in childhood and can easily remain with us throughout our entire lives. It does not matter whether you are five years old or fifty years old, this type of jealousy can still strike.

This type of jealousy can easily make you feel awful and it is fairly common to not be certain how to handle it.

Along the same lines, you may experience jealousy because of the way someone else looks. You may feel as though your looks do not measure up that of someone else you know and that as a result, you are not as worthy. This is an extremely common form of jealousy and it is one that drives people to go on diets and have cosmetic surgery in an effort to try to change the way they look. The problem is that this can become obsessive behavior in which you never reach a point where you feel satisfied with the way you look. This can truly be a problem because there is a good chance that there will always be at least one person who is better looking than you, thinner than you, etc. This is why it is imperative that we learn how to recognize jealousy and overcome it. Otherwise, it is easy to engage in very destructive behavior that can ruin your life.

# Loss Related Jealousy

Jealousy can also stem from loss in your life. There are three types of losses that you can experience which can result in jealousy. They are:

1. The loss of a friend to someone else
2. The loss of a romantic relationship to someone else
3. The loss of a loved one who has died

# Losing a Friend

As we mature and grow as people, it is not that uncommon for friendship to simply fizzle out. The feelings of closeness that we experience with friends can begin to fade over time as we develop into different people. When this transformation takes place the person who was once your good friend may replace your friendship with someone who has interests that are more similar to their own at that point in time. In order for an individual to have a solid foundation in life, friendships are crucial. As a result of this, emotions can take a heavy toll if you feel as though you have lost a friend or you are at risk for losing an important friendship. For example, you may ask yourself whether the new friend is somehow better than you.

# Loss of Romantic Relationships

While we often think they should, romantic relationships simply do not always last. Regardless of the legal status or duration of your relationship, when you find out that your significant other has found someone else, you may likely feel jealous. You may feel jealousy even if the relationship has already ended and you thought that you were over the other person. Once you realize that he or she has moved on to begin a romantic relationship with someone else, you may begin to experience feelings of jealousy. These feelings may begin as you start to question why your relationship with that person did not work out. You could easily ask yourself the same questions over and over, such as what the other person has that you don't and whether the other person is more attractive than you are. You may wonder why your ex does things with the new person that they never did with you.

Such questions may continue to bombard your mind until you feel as though you cannot escape them. You may feel the desire to lash out and uncover the answers to those questions. These types of feelings are most common right after a relationship has ended.

# Loss of a Loved One who Has Died

Whenever you are mourning someone you love who has died, jealousy may not be the first thing that you think of, but once the first phase of grieving has passed, you may begin to experience a pain whenever you think of other people who have not experienced the same type of loss as you. For example, if you lose your parents at a young age, you may experience jealousy whenever you hear others talk about the activities they share with their parents. This type of jealousy can easily begin to fester anytime you must hear about the good times that others have experienced with their loved ones.

Loss can result in more emotions than simply jealousy. It can also cause sorrow and grief. It is critical that you learn how to cope with jealousy during your life in order to avoid having your life taken over by it. Remember that while you may not be able to change the way you reacted to jealousy in the past, you can change the way you respond in the future.

# Cheating and Betrayal

Perhaps more than anything else, the fear of betrayal can cause extreme pain. This is because of the amount of ourselves that we devote to relationships and making them work. People commonly spend energy, time and even determination in trying to make a relationship work and last. When the person you love cheats on you, the feelings of hurt and betrayal can be severe. Infidelity can not only cause feelings of jealousy, but can also result in the end of a relationship.

Even if the relationship does not end and you do try to make the relationship work, jealousy can appear months or even years later on. You may even think that you have dealt with the situation and have come to accept it when those feelings begin to pop up again and the vicious cycle will begin all over again. This cycle can last for days and possibly for even weeks or years if you do not know how to cope with the feelings of jealousy.

Although you may feel as though you simply want to shut everyone out and lock yourself away from everyone when you experience these feelings of jealousy, this will simply do not good. It will only drive you and others around you crazy. The only way to really cope with these feelings of jealousy and betrayal is to learn how to overcome them once and for all.

# Chapter 2

# Why People Feel Jealousy

In the preceding chapter we discussed some of the most common things that can make people feel the emotion of jealousy. Now, it is time for us to examine precisely why people experience jealousy. All emotions are extremely complex and in order for us to truly understand those experiences, we must dig into the driving force behind those emotions. It is imperative to uncover the underlying causes in order to get over jealousy and put it behind you.

A number of different factors can play into why we feel jealousy. They include biological, psychological and environmental factors. Have you ever stopped to wonder why it is that you may experience jealousy more so than someone else? The reason lies in the way that the brain processes information. Each person is different and unique. Hormones vary from one person to another. While one person may be able to quickly put aside feelings of jealousy, it may not be so easy for another person and the reason is because of the way their brain functions.

We are going to take a look at several of the most common reasons why people become jealous in certain situations or toward others.

# Lack of Satisfaction

It is simply human nature to want more than we currently have. There is actually nothing wrong with wanting more than your current situation, but when you feel as though your life is somehow incomplete, feelings of jealousy can easily develop.

One of the primary reasons why people become jealous is due to lack of satisfaction with what they currently have. Let's take a look at a few examples that relate to this in order to better understand it.

At some point or another, everyone has experienced jealousy toward someone else. This is fairly common in a professional setting where you may experience jealousy toward a co-worker. Suppose for a moment you have put a lot of time and effort into your job, but it is the person who sits next to you who continually receives all of the credit? How would that make you feel? Probably angry and jealous as well. If you arrive early and leave late each day, but your supervisor promotes someone else ahead of you, it is only natural for you to experience and some strong emotions and one of those is likely to be jealousy. You may be jealous of the money, recognition, increased vacation time or better office that your co-worker receives. These are all things that everyone desires. You may be angry that you are not appreciated within your job, but there is also likely to be a big part of you that feels jealous that you do not have the same things as others.

This all relates to a lack of satisfaction that is driving the jealousy that you experience. These emotions can become so strong that they can easily build up until they boil over.

When you feel a lack of satisfaction in what you have, it can feel as though there is a big hole in your life that has not been fulfilled.

You may also experience this lack of satisfaction in personal relationships. For example, suppose that you see everyone around you involved in a serious relationship, perhaps even getting married and starting families. You want to experience that same kind of happiness, but it just is not happening for you. This is where the jealousy begins. Each time you see a couple walking down the street holding hands, you feel envy. This all relates to a lack of satisfaction with your own love life.

You may even be involved in a relationship, but if that relationship is unhappy, you may want more than what you have. You could be in between relationships and simply want to be with someone have someone with whom you can share special moments. During situations like these, you may very well feel jealous of others who are in relationships when you want the same thing and do not have it for yourself.

Of course, these other people are not to blame for your emotions and feelings. It's not their fault, but the force that is driving the rage you feel when you see them happy when you are not is a direct result of the fact that your needs are not being met.

## Understanding Rage

We previously touched on the fact that jealous feelings can stem from biological, psychological and environmental influences. The psychological aspect of your personality as well as the environment in which you were raised can both lead to issues of control. While you may not be completely responsible for your emotions, there are some techniques that you can use in order to overcome these emotions that you feel.

If you are a controlling person by nature you are probably going to be at a much higher risk for experiencing jealousy than someone who is not naturally a controlling person. When a person likes to be in control of everything around them, they may feel as though everything around them is coming apart is they sense they are not in control of a particular situation or even of another person. When they begin to sense they are not in complete control, it is common to develop fear and anxiety because they may feel as though they are going to lose something important to them.

Such controlling tendencies can be present in romantic relationships, in the workplace and with friends and family members. When you feel as though you are losing control, it is common for feelings of jealousy and even rage to begin. If these emotions are not kept in check, such jealous rages can lead to violence and destruction.

# Understanding Trust

We all know that infidelity can lead to jealousy. When you dig a bit deeper; however, it is really the lack of trust that resulted in the cheating that can cause you to feel jealous. If you feel as though you can no longer trust the other person because they have been unfaithful to you, it is not unusual to find yourself questioning every little thing that person does in the aftermath.

For example, if your partner is friends with someone else, you may wonder if there is really something else going on. You may even question relationships that person has in the workplace. You may see other people as a direct threat to your relationship with your partner.

This lack of trust, if not appropriately addressed, will continue to fester. You may even find that your partner simply glancing at someone else can be enough to set off feelings of jealousy. If you are not able to learn how to trust your partner again, such feelings of jealousy will continue until they eventually destroy your relationship.

# Understanding Self Esteem

Before you can begin to look to other people for causing your feelings of jealousy, you must first look inside yourself. You absolutely must feel confident in who you are or you are likely going to be at risk for feelings of jealousy. For example, if you feel you are not good enough or you do not look attractive enough then you are naturally going to feel jealous of others around you.

People who have low self esteem are naturally going to be more at risk for feeling jealousy than people who are confident. You may begin to feel jealous others around you because you feel they are in a better place than you, even if that is not the case. Such feelings are a direct result of a lack of confidence in yourself and are not really caused by other people.

You must feel secure with your own self and your own relationships. If this is not the case, it is not unlikely that you will begin to experience jealousy toward others who are secure with themselves and with their own lives.

# Chapter 3

# Entitlement and Reality

Entitlement and reality also play a strong role in jealousy and overcoming it. Whenever you feel a sense of entitlement, it is often caused by environmental factors with which you grew up. For example, if you grew up in a situation in which you received everything you wanted, what do you suppose will happen when you no longer get what you want from others around you?

It is completely natural to feel entitlement to certain things in life. For example, after working hard for several years and graduating college, it is normal to feel as though you are entitled to a good job. You may feel as though you are entitled to marriage when you spend years in a relationship with a significant other.

While those feelings are normal, if you feel that you are entitled to most things in life then you are likely going to feel jealousy when you do not get the things that you want, especially if others around you are getting the things you desire.

Such a sense of entitlement can also cause other problems within your life, including debt issues. When you see your friends getting all of the things out of life that you want, it can be tempting to go out and run up a lot of debt in order to acquire the same things. It can be easy to fail to realize in such situations that others may have worked for many years to acquire the material possessions they own.

This type of sense of entitlement can easily leave you feeling as though you are going without what you truly need in life. While the truth of the matter is that you do not typically need such material possessions in order to be happy, you may still feel entitled to them.

## Understanding Reality

Having unrealistic expectations regarding life can be one of the most dangerous types of jealousy. For example, suppose that you have made a career or life choice. If you have unrealistic expectations about that you may find yourself feeling jealousy towards others who have made other life or career choices. There is no getting around the fact that there are caps to all choices that you make. If you choose to stay at home for several years to raise your children and your family lives off one income, the reality is that you are probably not going to have as many material possessions as other families that have two incomes.

If you choose to be a teacher, you may very well have a rewarding career and enjoy your work, but the reality is that you are not going to make as much money as a surgeon or a lawyer and that means that you may not be able to afford an exotic location, luxury car or fancy home.

There are consequences to all choices that we make in life and we must be willing to accept the reality to those consequences in order to avoid jealousy. When we have unrealistic expectations, we are easily setting ourselves up for feelings of jealousy and unhappiness.

Of course, you can always take steps to change your circumstances in order to change your reality, but the fact is that you will need to either do that or accept the reality of your situation.

Unfortunately, many people have difficulty accepting that they are not able to have more than what they have at the moment.

Unrealistic expectations about life can also have a role in the jealous feelings that we experience in relationships with others. Suppose you are dating someone who clearly has commitment issues.

Even though you know this to be a fact, you may still expect that person to commit to you if that is what you desire. You may look forward to marrying that person one day and building a life with them, even though the person you are dating has no intention of taking those steps in life. In this case, such expectations would be completely unrealistic on your part.

It is possible to experience unrealistic expectations in all areas of your life, which can impact your well-being. You may experience jealousy when your best friend's child graduates from an Ivy League college and begins to pursue a successful career while your own child is content working for minimum wage. The important thing to note is that it is not realistic to expect that your children are going to be successful simply because someone else's child is.

You might also find yourself experiencing jealousy because someone else has been able to afford a lavish wedding or vacation. These feelings can be compounded if you work hard but you are not as financially well off as the other person and therefore cannot afford to pay for such niceties in life.

Such jealousy can easily begin to boil over inside of you. You may begin to experience rage towards others that you feel have more than you are better things in life than you. If you allow it and do not seek help, such rage and jealousy can take over your life and will eventually eat you up inside.

# Chapter 4

# The Consequences of Jealousy

Now that we understand a little bit about jealousy, it is time to take a look at some of the consequences of jealousy and what can happen in your life if you are not able to overcome those feelings of jealousy and move beyond them.

Even though you may not realize it, there is a good chance that those around you have noticed that you have not seemed yourself. They would probably like nothing more than to see you happy and to learn how to overcome jealousy. When you experience jealousy it not only affect your life but that of those around you as well.

If you are not able to overcome jealousy within your life, there are multiple consequences that can easily occur. They include:

1. Driving away people who are dear to you. When you are continually jealous, others may not wish to be around you.

2. Your career and work may be affected.

3. Your family life will be impacted.

4. Friendships will be affected.

5. Romantic relationships will be affected and could be ruined.

6. You will find it difficult to focus and concentrate, which can affect decision making skills.

7. You may be less able to trust others.

8. Family members, particularly kids, will develop a tendency toward jealousy.

9. You may not feel as energetic as you once did. Your health may even begin to suffer.

10. You may experience low self-esteem and a lack of confidence.

11. You may feel a lack of determination to get things done and achieve the things you want.

Jealousy can absolutely impact every aspect of your life. Instead of getting the things out of life that you want, jealousy will actually have the exact opposite effect on you.

Consider for a moment, does any of the following sound familiar to you?

- Have you noticed that friends and family do not call you as often as they once did?

- Was your last performance review at work as good as the previous review?

- Is your significant other always accusing you of being controlling?

- Do you feel as though you just never have fun anymore?

If any of these situations sound familiar, it is likely that you are experiencing the consequences of jealousy. If you are not able to get a handle on these feelings, it is only going to become worse. Now is the time to take charge of your emotions and your life and overcome this problem before it destroys your life.

# Chapter 5

# Techniques for Overcoming Jealousy

Overcoming jealousy is not as difficult as you might think it would be, but it will take some time and commitment on your part. In order for you to be able to begin living a life free of jealousy, you are going to need to be committed to recovery. There are five critical skills that you can use to overcome jealousy. They are:

- Positive thinking
- Facing reality
- Understanding comparison
- Elimination
- Acceptance

# Facing Reality

If there is one thing that you need to remember more than anything else, it is that everything is just what it is. You need to keep this in mind whenever you feel your mind being overtaken by feelings of jealousy. You must learn to accept the reality of situations and life to begin moving beyond jealousy. When you find yourself facing a situation that has the power to make you jealous, you must realize that there are really only two options open to you. You can either accept the situation for what it is or you can allow the jealousy to overtake you while you try to find some way to change the circumstances.

The second option is one which will typically lead you down a path of pain because as much as we want circumstances to change, wishing it does not make it so. You must come to understand that things simple are what they are and you have no control over certain things. It does not matter whether the jealousy you experience relates to material possessions, how much money you make or that someone you care about is with another person. It simply is what it is. The sooner you accept this reality the sooner you will be able to begin overcoming jealousy.

## Positive Thinking

People who are prone to jealousy tend to be far too hard on themselves. Instead of allowing jealousy to overtake your life look for positive things in your life and about yourself to focus upon. The reality is that you may not be as tall as you would like or make as much money as you want or live in the kind of house you have always dreamed of, but that does not mean that you do not have positive things in your life. Take a good, long look at your life and around you and you will probably find that your situation is not nearly as bad off as you might think.

You may not be as tall as your best friend, but you probably are not the shortest person in the world either. Perhaps you don't make a six figure income, but there are probably people who are worse off financially than you too. Unless you live in a complete hovel, your house probably is not that bad either.

Each time jealousy rears its ugly head, take a good look in the mirror and at your life and concentrate on the positive things in your life. Maybe you are not the gifted speaker that your co-worker is, but there is no doubt that you have other great qualities. Your co-worker may be able to speak wonderfully in public but isn't nearly as talented as you in another area. Everyone has their own unique gifts and qualities. Focus on yours. Think about the positive qualities that you have and stop worrying about those that you do not.

# Understanding Comparison

If there is one thing that you can do to quickly overcome jealousy, it is to stop comparing yourself to others. It can really easy to flip through a magazine or turn on the television and want to be as beautiful, glamorous or rich as the celebrities you see. Life can look life a fairytale when you're simply looking in from the other side. After watching a romantic comedy you may wonder why your partner isn't that romantic or sweet. In the same vein, it can also be incredibly easy to look at the lives of those around you and think that they have everything you want. The truth of the matter is that you are serving no purpose but to make yourself miserable when you continually compare yourself to others, whether it is someone on television or the neighbors down the street.

Stop and think about whether you really and truly want to be like everyone else? Sure, celebrities have a lot of money and when they appear on television and in magazines they look gorgeous. They also have no privacy and often have more personal troubles can you can count. Even your neighbors down the street who may appear to have the ideal life may have troubles that you are not aware of.

The reality is that everyone has their problems, even if you do not see them. You are a unique individual and you do not need to be like everyone else in order to have a good life and be happy. The sooner you cease comparing yourself to others, the easier it will be to overcome your jealousy.

So what if your neighbor down the street has a better car and home and money than you? Maybe they work so hard to pay for those things that they don't even have time to enjoy them. So what if your best friend's husband is seems so sweet and romantic? Maybe there are days when she wishes he was just like every other guy.

If you continually compare yourself to others, there is little doubt that you will judge your life and find it to be lacking in a variety of aspects. No one is equal. Not in looks, not in money, not in power or in anything else.

# Acceptance

Along with accepting the reality of a situation, you must also be prepared to accept who you are. The same is true of accepting the past. It can be hard to do this, especially if the past involves some sort of betrayal by someone you love. The truth is that you simply cannot control the actions of others. You also do not have the power to change things. You must be prepared each and every day to remember that you are not going to allow what has happened in the past to control your present.

This does take determination, but when you are able to accept this you will be in a much better position to overcome jealousy and stop allowing it to control your daily life. You must be strong willed in order for this to work. You must stop giving in to those feelings. It does take work, because oftentimes it is much easier to just give in rather than fight it but if you truly want to overcome jealousy you must be prepared to do this.

The simple truth is that you have to let go of the past.

# Elimination

This phase of overcoming jealousy can be somewhat difficult, but it is also necessary. To finally overcome jealousy, you must be prepared to eliminate areas in your life that are causing those jealous feelings to appear. This must be within reason, of course. If you are holding onto items from a past relationship because you are still hoping that things will change when the truth of the matter is that the other person has already moved on with their life, then you need to get those items out of your daily life. Put them away. Give them away. Stop focusing on them. Give yourself the space away from all of the memories that you need until you feel the jealousy begin to reside.

When possible, try to avoid going to places and being around people that cause those jealous feelings to bubble up to the top. While you should never consider cutting things or people out of your life for good, you do need to give yourself some time to heal. For example, stop going to same restaurants where you and your ex spent so many times. Eliminate the reminders and focus on other things that will keep you busy and active. After a period of time you will probably begin to see that the jealous feelings have begun to subside. At that point, you may well be able to begin gradually reintroducing those places and people to your life without feeling the jealousy at all.

The hardest thing of all can be to determine whether you need to try to salvage or end a relationship in which infidelity has occurred. This is a completely personal situation and only you know whether there is any real hope of trying to salvage that relationship, but if you have tried and you are still feeling continual jealousy and turmoil along with a lack of trust that your partner can be faithful, you may need to seriously consider whether it is perhaps time to end the relationship. A successful relationship simply cannot exist when there is such turmoil and jealousy present.

This is certainly not to say that someone who has been unfaithful is incapable of ever being faithful again but if you are simply not able to trust them again, then it may be time for you to move on.

When you experience these types of feelings in a romantic relationship, they are usually due to one of two problems. Either you are experiencing jealousy when the other person has really done nothing to deserve it or you are experiencing jealousy as a result of betrayal in the relationship. In either case, you have three options available to you.

1. You can remain in the relationship and the two of you can continue to hold onto the feelings of jealousy until the relationship finally terminates; in which case you will both probably walk away with a lot of baggage and carry those feelings over into subsequent relationships.

2. You can choose to end the relationship by both of you acknowledging the role that jealousy has played in the relationship and ultimately decide that you simply cannot remain in the relationship due to the amount of pain the jealousy has caused.

3. You can choose to heal the relationship. If you choose to do this you will both need to acknowledge the role of jealousy in the relationship, look at the relationship in an open and honest manner and decide that the relationship is important enough to both of you do get rid of the jealousy once and for all.

Certainly, none of these options are easy. They all require you to analyze the relationship and make a determination regarding whether you think the relationship can continue. If you decide that it is important enough for you to try to heal it, you must accept that you have not chosen an easy path and that both of you will need to dedicate yourselves to overcoming the issues that have caused problems in the past.

## When your Partner Has done Nothing to Warrant Jealousy

While in many cases jealousy can be caused due to an act of betrayal in a relationship that is not always the case. In some instances, you may feel yourself become overwhelmed by jealousy even when your partner has not done anything to warrant it. If that is the situation in which you find yourself, it is important for you to focus on the following guidelines:

1.  Take some time to yourself by getting away to take a walk. This is the time to work on calming down and reducing the intensity of your emotions. At this point you do not need to worry about trying to get rid of the feelings, but simply focus on toning them down.

2. Try taking some deep breaths if you find yourself feeling overwhelmed and anxious. This will help to clear your thinking and assist you in reducing the intensity of those emotions. When you are overwhelmed by the emotions you feel, it can be difficult to think clearly.

3. Do not even think about approaching your partner and attempting to repair any of the damage that has been caused in your relationship by your jealousy at this point. It is imperative that you take some time to acknowledge the role that jealousy has had in the relationship and recognize what the consequences of that jealousy have been. This is also a good time to look for patterns for this type of behavior in your life. If this has occurred over and over in your life, you must take the time to find out where it is stemming from in order to repair it.

4. You must also ask yourself whether you are willing to commitment to doing what is necessary in order to resolve these jealousy issues that have taken place in your life and to rebuild trust with your partner.

If you feel that you are willing to make that commitment, you must keep in mind that the other person must also be willing to make the same commitment. Both of you must be fully committed to healing the relationship. If, after analyzing this, you feel that you are not willing to do whatever is necessary to overcoming the issues of jealousy, then you must recognize that the prospect for this relationship as well as for overcoming your jealousy are bleak. The simple fact is that until you are fully committed to analyzing the feelings, thoughts and fears that are at the root of your jealousy, there is not going to be much chance for you to have a successful relationship because you will continue to repeat the same mistakes and behaviors over and over. Take the time right now to look at yourself and the situation and decide whether you can really commit to doing what is necessary to healing yourself and the relationship.

5. If you decide that you are able to do this, the next step is to put your commitment in writing. Make a commitment to yourself that you intend to rebuild the broken trust in the relationship and heal the jealousy. Remember that if you are not completely honest in this, then there is no point in completing the exercise because the actions you take will be of no benefit to anyone; either you or your partner.

6. The next step is to make a commitment to asking your partner for forgiveness for your jealous behavior and actions. Remember that simply telling the other person that you are sorry is probably not going to be enough to rebuild the relationship. You must ask them for their forgiveness and be prepared to tell them what you are going to do differently in the future.

7. Begin by making a list of exactly what you are going to do differently in your relationship and your life. Focus on the strategies that were previously presented.

8. Ask your partner to talk with you about the situation. If this has become a real issue in the relationship, you must accept that it could be difficult to get the other person to be willing to listen. Your partner may naturally have a lot of anger and it is quite likely that they will want to express how your actions and jealousy have hurt them. You must be prepared to listen as well as to understand their point of view and take responsibility for your own actions and the consequences of those actions.

9. Once you have listened to your partner, take the next step by telling them that you are completely commitment to rebuilding the trust in the relationship, repairing it and overcoming your jealousy.

10. If your partner is not willing to listen to you at this point, you may consider writing them a letter that expresses your feelings and in which you take responsibility for what you have done in the past and what you are willing to do change. Even if the other person is not willing to talk to you about these issues right now, you

must then begin to put those steps into action. You will find that once you begin to make positive changes within your life, all of your relationships will begin to show signs of improvement.

11. If the other person is willing to talk to you, remember that it is imperative that you do not become defensive or attempt to interrupt. This can be difficult as the other person may feel the need to go over the past and rehash everything again. You must allow them the opportunity to do this. Do not interrupt. Even if it seems as though they are repeating old news, it is important that you acknowledge the past and the pain your actions have caused and once again reiterate your willingness to make changes to heal the relationship.

12. Remember that you must be specific. Do not just say that you are willing to change. Tell the other person exactly what you are going to do to overcome your jealousy and heal the relationship.

You should be aware that when you make this type of commitment, there are many things to be considered. Before you commit to rebuilding the relationship and overcoming the jealousy, you must be certain that you truly have the desire to do so. You must believe that you can actually follow-through on the steps that are necessary to make those changes a reality.

In many instances, you may find that it is easier if you have a strong support system to assist you in making these changes. A support system can come from a variety of venues, such as a counselor, therapist or even a close friend. Making such changes to your life can be hard, especially if your jealous behavior has been ingrained in you for a long time. Having a friend or a counselor who can support you in changing your behavior can make it a bit easier.

You must also focus on learning new and more effective ways to communicate with your partner. These new skills are a strong part of making the necessary changes in your life that will allow you to rebuild trust and heal the relationship.

It is important to always ask the other person if they have a desire to rebuild the relationship. Never make assumptions. You cannot rebuild the relationship alone, even if it is your jealousy that has caused problems in the relationship. The other person must be willing to work toward rebuilding trust as well in order for the relationship to succeed. If they feel they cannot forgive you and they no longer have a desire to rebuild the relationship, you must unfortunately accept this as reality and realize that this is not something that you are able to control.

If the two of you decide that you do both have a desire to heal the relationship, you should put your commitments in writing and post them in conspicuous places where you will be able to see them each and every day. For example, post them on the fridge, in your car, on your desk, in your purse; anywhere that you will be able to frequently see them. Make sure that you review them frequently and especially anytime that you feel as though you are slipping back into your old habits.

It is also imperative that you stick to all of your commitments and agreements. The only way that you can truly change is to make sure that you keep to those commitments. It can be a slow process and feel as though you are only taking one step at a time, but this is critical for achieving real change. It is essential that you demonstrate that you mean to keep your word to your partner. If you are able to do this, it will allow them to see that you are making progress.

Anytime that you experience insecurities and doubts, rather than engaging in what is certain to be a painful discussion with your partner, simply explain that you are feeling insecure.

Not everyone is able to move past issues of jealousy within a relationship. When that happens, the relationship will usually dissolve, but it is important that you not give up on making the changes that are necessary. Perhaps you were not able to salvage this relationship, but if you continue to work toward making effective changes, you will be able to apply what you have learned to future relationships.

# When your Partner Has Betrayed You

When one or both partners in a relationship has done something for there to be a legitimate lack of trust, such as a betrayal, it is only natural for feelings of jealousy to emerge. While this can be difficult situation in which to find yourself, it is important to recognize that it is possible to heal the relationship and overcome the lack of trust and feelings of jealousy if you are both willing to commit to making that happen.

1. Begin by making sure that both of you have had a chance to calm down. Anytime there is a betrayal in a relationship, emotions tend to run high. It is difficult, if not impossible to make any type of progress when emotions are intense. Try some deep breathing and perhaps even take the opportunity for both of you to have some space to clear your mind and tone down the emotions.

2. Take some time for both of you to analyze how you feel about the relationship and what you want out of the relationship. It is a good idea at this point for both of

you to spend some time to yourself. The amount of time that you need may depend upon the intensity of your emotions. Be prepared for the fact that the other person may need more time. Some people may only need a few minutes but others may need much longer. Be patient and be prepared to give your partner the time and space they need.

3. During this time consider what you want out of the relationship. Remember that there are really only three options when you find yourself in this type of situation. You can choose to remain in the relationship, along with all of the blame, fears and judgments; you can choose to end the relationship or you can choose to try to heal the relationship.

4. If you decide that you want to try to heal the relationship, both of you must be committed to this. You must both be willing to do whatever is necessary for healing the relationship. If that is the case, it can be helpful to make a written statement of your commitment. This could entail ask-

ing the other person for their forgiveness. Even if you feel as though you are the victim, it may mean that you must be ready to sit down and take a look at whether you had any role in creating a situation where there was a lack of trust. Look at whether you could perhaps have been a better partner.

5. If you were the person in the relationship who created the lack of trust, you must make a commitment to asking the other person for their forgiveness and also for making amends for your behavior of the past. Remember that simply saying you are sorry at this point will likely not be enough to repair the situation and heal the relationship.

6. If you are the victim in this situation and you find yourself exhibiting jealous behavior when you never have before, you must take some time to analyze what changes need to be made in the relationship. This is assuming, of course, that your partner is willing to make changes and truly wants to make amends for their behavior.

7. It is important to keep in mind that the only way that you can truly make amends is to find out what changes the other persons desires and then for both of you to honestly ask yourselves whether those changes will improve the relationship. Keep in mind that what you may believe to be appropriate to make amends in the relationship may not necessarily be enough for the other person, depending upon their point of view.

8. Take the time needed to talk to one another and discuss the situation. Make sure that you both have an opportunity to discuss your feelings. Do not interrupt while the other person is talking. This may well be difficult if one of you is feeling very hurt and possibly even angry. The partner who has caused the betrayal must be willing to listen and attempt to understand the other person's viewpoint. They must also be willing to admit to what they have done to cause the feelings of mistrust in the relationship.

9. Both of you should discuss how you would like the relationship to evolve and what changes will be necessary in order for that to happen. Keep in mind that if one of you is still stuck in a position where you are assessing blame, it will be impossible to rebuild the trust in your relationship. You must both be willing to take an honest look at how you would like your relationship to be and what you need to do to get it there.

Remember that you may need to seek help from a counselor or therapist. Changing behavior can be difficult and there is nothing wrong with seeking help from someone to support as you go about the process.

Make an effort to keep to all commitments that you make. If you make a commitment and do not keep to it, it will be impossible to rebuild trust and you will be starting all over again.

It is not always possible to rebuild a relationship when there has been an act of betrayal. If you are both not willing to work toward resolving the issues and rebuilding the trust, there is little hope for the relationship. Even if you are willing to work at it, if the other person is not, there is nothing that you can do about this. It falls into the category of accepting what is reality and then moving on. Take what you have learned and apply it to future relationships.

# Conclusion

Overcoming jealousy is not easy, but you must be willing to tackle it head on and make the changes that are necessary in order to overcome it. You should be aware that nothing happens overnight and the changes that are needed to overcome jealousy will not be immediate, but with time, patience and commitment, it is possible to get there.

The consequences of continuing to have your life ruled by jealousy can be severe. Now is the time to make a commitment to a fresh start and tackling the changes that will allow you to live a happier and more fulfilling life, free of jealousy.

# Appendix 1

In many instances, jealousy can seem to be triggered by certain things. Learning to recognize those triggers is essential to learning to overcome jealousy. Take a few moments to stop and think about the things that seem to trigger your jealousy.

_____
_____
_____
_____
_____
_____
_____
_____
_____
_____
_____
_____
_____
_____
_____
_____
_____
_____
_____
_____
_____

There may also be times when you can recognize certain things in yourself that tends to cause your jealousy to rise to the surface. For example, if you feel stressed or overwhelmed you may be more prone to feeling jealous.

_____

_____

_____

_____

_____

_____

_____

_____

_____

_____

_____

_____

_____

_____

_____

_____

_____

_____

_____

_____

_____

# Appendix 2

In many instances, things that have happened in the past can continue to affect you in the present. This is certainly true of jealousy. Complete the following worksheet to determine whether there may be things in our past that are continuing to have an affect on you now.

- When did you first begin to notice that jealousy was an issue for you? Did this occur within a relationship that exists now or perhaps in a previous relationship? Describe the situation.

_____
_____
_____
_____
_____
_____
_____
_____
_____
_____
_____
_____
_____
_____
_____

- Can you describe anything regarding your current relationship and situation that seems familiar or similar to other situations or relationships? It is important to keep in mind that in many cases, jealousy issues can reach far back into the past and could even go back as far as your relationship with your parents and/or siblings.

_____

_____

_____

_____

_____

_____

_____

_____

_____

_____

_____

_____

_____

_____

_____

_____

_____

_____

_____

_____

- Can you recognize any patterns that may emerge as you consider past relationships and your current situation?

_____

_____

_____

_____

_____

_____

_____

_____

_____

_____

_____

_____

_____

_____

_____

_____

_____

_____

_____

_____

_____

# Appendix 3

Jealousy can often pop up when we least expect it. When that happens, it is important to be able to sit down and analyze your feelings before you allow them to take control of your life. This worksheet is designed to help you do just that.

- Describe your thoughts of jealousy at this moment in time.......

_____

_____

_____

_____

_____

_____

_____

_____

_____

_____

_____

_____

_____

_____

_____

_____

- Think about the emotions you have just described and now take look at what is really at the root of those thoughts and feelings…..

_____

_____

_____

_____

_____

_____

_____

_____

_____

_____

_____

_____

_____

_____

_____

_____

_____

_____

_____

_____

_____

_____

- Recognizing that you do not have to remain captive to these feelings is critical. Consider new ways that you can act and think in such situations.

_____
_____
_____
_____
_____
_____
_____
_____
_____
_____
_____
_____
_____
_____
_____
_____
_____
_____
_____
_____
_____

# Appendix 4

When you have exhibited signs of jealousy in a relationship, it is important to work on rebuilding trust. Saying I'm sorry simply is not enough in most circumstances. You must be willing to offer a sincere apology and ask for the other person's forgiveness. This is the first step in rebuilding trust in any relationship. This worksheet will help you to do that.

• Describe how you would begin to apologize to the person in your life who has been affected by your jealousy.

_____

_____

_____

_____

_____

_____

_____

_____

_____

_____

_____

_____

_____

_____

- What steps can you take to demonstrate to that person that you are willing to change your behavior and rebuild trust?

_____
_____
_____
_____
_____
_____
_____
_____
_____
_____
_____
_____
_____
_____
_____
_____
_____
_____
_____
_____
_____
_____
_____

# Appendix 5

Learning new communication skills is essential when you want to re-establish trust in a relationship and change destructive behavior to improve that relationship. This means that you must be able to communicate your feelings and what you want in a clear manner. Before you can communicate them to your partner, you must be able to recognize them yourself.

- Describe what you are feeling right now. Be sure to listen to your body because it will often give you clues as to your feelings, such as tension, tightness, pain, fluttering, etc.

_____
_____
_____
_____
_____
_____
_____
_____
_____
_____
_____
_____
_____
_____

- Now, take a moment to identify the emotions you are feeling. Below, write down the feelings that you have been able to identify by listening to your body.

_____

_____

_____

_____

_____

_____

_____

_____

_____

_____

_____

_____

_____

_____

_____

_____

_____

_____

_____

_____

_____

_____

_____

_____

- Take a few moments now to translate those feelings into words, such as "I feel angry about.........." Or "I am afraid about............."

_____

_____

_____

_____

_____

_____

_____

_____

_____

_____

_____

_____

_____

_____

_____

_____

_____

_____

_____

_____

_____

_____

# Appendix 6

Taking responsibility for your own emotions and actions is essential to changing your behavior, overcoming jealousy and getting what you want out of life. Answer the following questions.

• "How can I take more responsibility for my own life?"

_____

_____

_____

_____

_____

_____

_____

_____

_____

_____

_____

_____

_____

_____

_____

_____

_____

_____

_____

_____

- What ideas or attitudes do I need to change to move forward with my life?

_____

_____

_____

_____

_____

_____

_____

_____

_____

_____

_____

_____

_____

_____

_____

_____

_____

_____

_____

_____

_____

_____

_____

_____

# Free Online Seduction Course
## For Men

As a thank you for buying this book, I would like to give you access to my online women seduction course.

To claim your free spot, please go to
**www.foreverlaid.com**
and enter your valid email address now.

# Also by Taylor Timms

## Beautiful Breasts Pictures
ISBN 978-1-926917-01-6

## Top Bikini Pictures
ISBN 978-0-9866426-3-0

## Forever Laid Formula
Best Ways To Get Women To Sleep With You
ISBN 978-0-9866004-2-5

## Best Gift Ideas For Women
Perfect Gifts Ideas For Any Special Occasion
ISBN 978-0-9866004-4-9